Alpha to Omega 7

Robinson

Daniel Defoe

Retold by Gillian Oxford

A Birkbeck Oxford Series

Heinemann

Heinemann Educational Publishers
Halley Court, Jordan Hill, Oxford OX2 8EJ
A division of Reed Educational and Professional Publishing Ltd

OXFORD MELBOURNE AUCKLAND
JOHANNESBURG BLANTYRE GABORONE
IBADAN PORTSMOUTH (NH) USA CHICAGO

03 02
10 9 8 7 6 5 4 3

ISBN 0 435 10443 8

Designed and produced by Artistix
Illustrations by Mike Lacey
Cover design by Artistix
Printed and bound in the UK by Thomson Litho Ltd

Tel: 01865 888058 email: info.he@heinemann.co.uk

Robinson Crusoe

Robinson Crusoe was born in York in England in 1632. His father did not want him to go to sea, but when Crusoe was eighteen years old, he ran away from home. He got a job as a sailor and went off on a ship to Africa. He became a merchant, selling toys and souvenirs from England. He was paid in gold dust.

One day, Crusoe took a ship to Brazil in South America. In Brazil, he saw that the way to get rich was to buy a plantation, so he used his gold dust to buy land. He became a planter, growing sugar cane and tobacco.

The planters needed workers to look after the crops on their land, so Crusoe set out on a ship to Africa, to buy slaves.

The shipwreck

The sea can be very dangerous. Sailing boats sink each year. The big sailing ships of the past were often wrecked.

When Crusoe set out, the sky was clear. But soon storm clouds began to gather. The wind got stronger and stronger. Crusoe's ship was blown on to a sandbank near an island. There was a loud crash. Water began to pour into the ship.

The sailors got into a small boat, but it was smashed to bits by the endless waves. Crusoe found a plank of wood and held fast. He was washed safe ashore and then he knew no more.

When he awoke, the sun was out. He was on a beautiful, green island. He looked around but no one else was there. He called out, but there was no reply. All his shipmates had drowned. He was the only one alive.

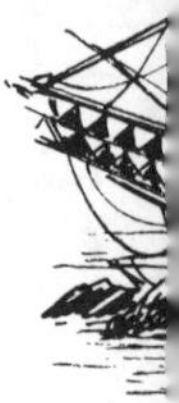

The island

Luck was still with him. There were no dangerous animals or even flies on the island.

He swam out to the wrecked ship and found tools, nails and wood. He took them back to the island. Then he went back to the ship and got guns, canvas and rope. He even found the ship's dog, who was full of joy to see him, and a cat. He made many trips to the ship to get everything he needed.

When he had got all his tools, Crusoe made a tent from canvas. He also made a table and a chair from wood. He started a garden where he grew grapes, bananas and other fruit. He built a fence around his tent 'castle', which was wide and strong. He climbed over his fence with a ladder. When he was inside the fence he felt safe.

Crusoe caught some goats and kept them as pets. They gave him milk for butter and cheese. When he needed new clothes, he made a hat and a coat from goat's skin. He even made an umbrella from goat's skin to shade him from the sun. There was no winter, but there was a time when it rained and rained.

As the years went by, Crusoe came to like the island. He grew corn and rice from some grain he had found on the ship. He learnt how to make bread. He had fruit from his garden. His grapes dried in the sun and became sweet raisins. He made clay pots for water.

Crusoe wrote a diary and kept a note of the days as the weeks, months and years went by.

Man Friday

One day, after eighteen years alone, Crusoe had a shock. He saw a man's footprint in the sand. Whose could it be? Perhaps it was someone from the war-like tribes on the mainland; cannibals who ate their captives.

He took his gun and crept down the hill. He hid in the trees near the beach. To his horror, he saw a group of men around a fire. Another man was tied up, captive. It was clear that the others were going to cook and eat him.

But when the men came to take the captive to the fire, he broke free. The man ran up the hill into the trees where Crusoe was hiding. Two of the other men chased him.

Crusoe rushed to help the man. He aimed his gun at the other men and shot. One man fell and then another. The men on the beach ran to their canoe and jumped into it. Soon they were far away.

Crusoe made signs to the man he had saved and led him to his tent. He fed the man and began to teach him English words. He called the man 'Friday' because he came on a Friday.

It was a comfort to have a friend on the island.

Escape from the island

Crusoe had been on the island for twenty-eight years when he and Man Friday saw a ship. The ship's crew wanted to leave their captain on the island to die. But Crusoe and Man Friday untied the captain in the night and took him back to his ship. All the crew were asleep on the island, so Crusoe, Man Friday and the captain sailed the ship away. They left all the crew behind.

They sailed the ship back to Brazil. When they got to Brazil, Crusoe found that his plantation had done very well. He had become a rich man. He gave money to all who had helped him. Then he and Man Friday set sail for England.

When they got to England, Crusoe found that his father had died long ago. He was very sad that he had not seen his father again, but he found he had two nephews. Both of them wanted to go to sea, but they didn't have any money. Crusoe helped them to do what they wanted.

Over the next few years, Crusoe married and had children. His best friend, Man Friday, also stayed with him. Crusoe was very happy in England with his family, but he could never forget the sea. He wanted to see his island one more time before he died.

When he told his nephew this, his nephew wanted to take him back to the island on his ship. Crusoe was now very old, but he and Man Friday went with his nephew back to the island.

There were many people on the island now. Crops of corn and rice, from the grain that Crusoe had planted all those years ago, were growing well.

Crusoe felt that his father would have been proud of him. He always thanked God for his good fortune.

Word list

This story is suitable for use when pupils have reached page 147 of the *Alpha to Omega Handbook.*

There are a number of words in the story that are taught beyond page 147 of the *Alpha to Omega Handbook.* Those that students may find difficult to *read* are included in the 'Harder words' list below.

Words and phrases special to the story

1 Ro/bin/son Crusoe
2 A/fri/ca
3 merchant
4 Brazil
5 South A/me/ri/ca
6 plan/ta/tion
7 planter
8 sugar cane
9 to/bac/co
10 slaves
11 tribes
12 can/ni/bals
13 captives
14 Man Friday

Harder words

1 eighteen
2 sailor
3 sou/ve/nirs
4 dan/ger/ous
5 island
6 beau/ti/ful
7 an/i/mals
8 ban/an/as
9 caught
10 um/bre/lla
11 horror
12 comfort
13 nephews
14 married
15 children